Dragon in my Purse

poems by

Betsy Littrell

Finishing Line Press
Georgetown, Kentucky

Dragon in my Purse

Copyright © 2021 by Betsy Littrell
ISBN 978-1-64662-664-9 First Edition
All rights reserved under International and Pan-American Copyright Conventions. No part of this book may be reproduced in any manner whatsoever without written permission from the publisher, except in the case of brief quotations embodied in critical articles and reviews.

ACKNOWLEDGMENTS

The author would like to thank the following publications in which these poems first appeared, sometimes in different versions:

Swimming with Elephants: "Memory by Scent"
Prometheus Dreaming: "Lauren"
Literary Mama: "March 19, 2003"
Hummingbird: "Dragon in my Purse" (formerly "The Power of the Dragon")
The Write Launch: "Elegy to the Queen of Hearts"
Westchester Review: "Row 12, Seat A"
Broad River Review: "Backwash"
Several poems also appeared in the author's first book, *This Woman is Haunted*.

Publisher: Leah Huete de Maines
Editor: Christen Kincaid
Cover Art: Nicholas Littrell
Author Photo: Zachary Michael Photography
Cover Design: Elizabeth Maines McCleavy

Order online: www.finishinglinepress.com
also available on amazon.com

Author inquiries and mail orders:
Finishing Line Press
PO Box 1626
Georgetown, Kentucky 40324
USA

Table of Contents

March 19, 2003 1

The Black Dress 2

Soaking 3

Lauren 4

Dragon in my Purse 5

Elegy to the Queen of Hearts 6

Teaching My Son to Drive 7

Guilt 8

Row 12, Seat A 9

Green-eyed Boy 10

In the Form of Flowers 11

Copacetic 12

Joshua 13

Aging without Grace 14

Unplugged 16

Backwash 17

January 18

Anxiety 19

Butterfly in the Window 20

Combat Hunger 21

Guide Words 22

Memory by Scent 23

To Iain
All of your words are like poems to me.

To Joshua, Gabriel, Nicholas and Kellen
I am blessed.

We need to understand the power and powerlessness embodied in motherhood in patriarchal culture.
—Adrienne Rich

March 19, 2003

Seven-pound dark-haired baby
nursing from my breast,

half drinking, half dreaming,
while I wonder if his dad

will ever hold him. Orange
and red raindrops fall from

the sky as I sit, not blinking,
in my brown chair. My husband

presses a black button with his thumb
from the back seat of his

jet, releases a missile
that kills an *enemy*,

a child? The distance from the cloud
to the ground too great to

know what's ablaze. Is that fireball
heading for his plane? I try to breathe

but the air won't leave my lungs.
The two of us—new mother,

sleepy baby, bonded to this brown chair,
watching the world burn.

The Black Dress

My body molded
to my bed,
long, brown hair fanned
behind me,

I sang hymns
in the house of God today.
I cooked a customary
Sunday roast beef,

and I wear a black dress.

My eyes are open windows,
letting the chill in,
and I ache to close them.
I stare at the blank ceiling,

in my black dress.

I shop for groceries,
scrub floors,
flip pancakes for the
children's breakfast,
that makes them happy,

while I wear a black dress.

My skin feels soft, sensual.
I contort my body
into triangle shapes—
become a warrior—
in yoga.
Now I lie motionless.

Beautiful in my black dress.

When I do cartwheels,
I will still wear
my black dress.

Soaking

Lavender and chamomile fizzing
from bubbles, I'm staring

at the white tiles, rectangles,
figuring out their different

patterns. It reminds me of
hopscotch chalked on

pavement or a carefully crafted
cobblestone street. Who knew

there were so many shades
of white? Maybe it's just natural

variations, or it could be the lighting
in this room. Delicate water droplets

from the steamy bath may have
grayed the milky white, or my eyes

are playing tricks on me.
Maybe they're all the same.

I think about how I have to call
the school and let them know

my son is sick,
but it's all a lie. I wonder

how long I can sit here, skin
pruning, until the next thought

interrupts my peace.
I'm so thirsty.

Lauren

I wanted to plop backwards in the
snow and wave my arms and legs
up and down, making a snow angel

next to you. I wanted to read *Where the Wild Things Are*
with a flashlight under a blanket fort with
you. I wanted to run with you through a

meadow, picking every dandelion,
blowing seeds in the wind.
I wanted to jump the waves, holding

your hand, while we looked for sand
dollars together. Instead, there was
blood, and somebody must have yanked

the bones from my body because I
crumpled into a lifeless heap of flesh on
the linoleum floor.

I swear I smell
baby powder. And a friend
left flowers on the porch.

Dragon in my Purse

I found a dragon
in my purse. Wrinkled,
I wasn't sure if it was stuck
at the bottom of my black
and white bag for weeks
or months. Sharp teeth,
strong wings, scales
all down his back
to protect him in his journey,
wherever he might land,
erasure marks inside
the legs, horns and tail.
I can feel my son's
9-year-old arms wrap
around my waist as I study
this art, clutch
my chest, sink to the floor,
and I imagine him slowly
perfecting each detail
as he makes his way through
the flames of this world.

Elegy to the Queen of Hearts

You stumbled, fell on the plane,
your sister explaining that
you were ok despite your
bloody knee—you just sometimes
lost your balance. I was 5 months

along with my next son and you parked your
hand on my belly—the only
thing you wanted to feel
was new life growing inside
me. I come to see you this time.

I bring the baby that
had lived in my belly, the
one you told me I needed,
and I nurse in a room next
to your casket. I say goodbye

and my son wraps his hand
around my pinky finger.

Teaching My Son to Drive

I calmly demand that he stay in the
left lane. Saturday morning, 3,500-pound steel machine,
I use my calm voice - really I do - *You're too far to the right,*
I say, no shake in my voice. I try not to be a jerk or to

jerk the wheel as another car merges and he doesn't
know whether to press the gas pedal or brake.
Our 20-minute journey too fast,
too slow is nearly over as we exit. *A long beeeep*

and he tries to move to the turn lane. *You've got to look all
around you!* We make it to safety, just one
angry horn along the way.

Guilt

She missed two
soccer games today.
Her youngest had his first
loose tooth. Did it come out
while she was gone? Her third-grader still
wet the bed. Was it anxiety? She wore a dress
with pockets, left one weighted down
with stones. Her 13-year-old,
quiet. Ignored? Her oldest, a mama's boy,
on anti-depressants already. She takes
the stones from her pocket, writes
No on every one,
sucks the dirt off
in the side of her cheek
and places the wet stones
in her right pocket.

Row 12, Seat A

I was a little drunk
after some chardonnay
at the airport bar where
I had slouched on a stool, legs
crossed, grading
essays in purple ink. Now on the
plane, it was not
full, and there was an empty
seat between me and some
stranger. I didn't want to
flip through a magazine
found in the seat back pocket,
listen to top hits of the 1980s,
or chit-chat with my row-mate.
I wanted a moment in my
window seat to enjoy my rare
inebriation, to let my mind
sift through sand for rubies
in the extra gray-leather space. I
wanted to gaze out the window,
to dream of leaping
onto Mars where I would
lay in its red dust alone,
making dirt angels visible
by telescope before returning,
ready to sober up.
So when the stranger began to
speak, I fantasized that I
punched him in his chubby nose;
instead, I blabbered
about how my sister
is becoming my brother,
and how my mother won't
call him his preferred name.

Green-eyed Boy

Green-eyed boy, I worry about you.
You're a whisper in a thunderstorm

and I can't always hear your
words. Behind closed doors,

you protect yourself, or maybe
hide, from big lightning strikes

just outside your window. I want
you to know that it's ok to ask

me to be your shelter,
even though you must raise your voice

over the howling winds.
Straight As and soccer goals are not

what I love about you—
it's just you and what I can see

in your eyes. Don't be afraid
to drink the rain drops from the sky.

In the Form of Flowers

Mom bought me blonde-headed Barbies and
Cabbage Patch dolls dressed in lavender
and flowers, smelling of baby powder,
but she knew how to pile on the guilt like
weeks of unfolded laundry.

I dial her number, and I can picture
her in bed in a floral
nightgown when she says in her
Massachusetts accent, *I haven't heard
from you in a while.* And then she tells me,
legs dangling off her mattress,
that her grandchildren are growing
up without knowing her. I imagine her
running her fingers through her dyed-blonde hair,
*Why don't you come for a visit? It's been
too long.* This conversation answers
her questions in my mind.

Yes, she's getting older and can
never remember where she put that
birthday card she bought me, although
she does remember to complain about
my sister's haircut or to tell me Billy is divorced again,
but I really must find a florist
and send her some carnations,
ruffled ones with pink edges.

Copacetic

It drives my partner crazy,
the way he thinks I pick

eggs from a carton. Maybe it
looks like I'm blindfolded and grab

the first egg I touch, even
if it's in the middle of the dozen.

He likes order—pick the eggs
from front to back. I, too,

am methodical. First, the freckled
ones, or maybe the ones not

quite ovular. Sometimes I snatch
the runt of the litter or

the one a lighter shade of brown
than the others. Deciding

which egg will become part
of my recipe brings me back

to middle school, waiting to be
adopted on a P.E. basketball team,

selected last because I was short.
I want to live my life

finding beauty in the imperfect,
creating disorder wherever I go.

Joshua

He left his fingerprint on the
moon then glided through space,
back to Earth, back to his room,
door closed, nobody having known
he even left. He returned
with stars in his brain that didn't
quite touch and turned off
at the wrong times. He wished
for a switch so he would
keep shining. Instead, he popped
a pink pill, sat on his bed and
remembered touching the moon, his
secret he didn't wish to keep.

Aging without Grace

My mother called to tell me
that she hates my hair. My response —

I don't care. I've changed
my hair color four different times

in the four months since I turned
forty. From brown to

blonde highlights to auburn to
scarlet. It's my way of

rebelling against my age. *Everybody*
told me to cut my mane once I hit

the forty mark, that my long hair
would drag my face down. I'm keeping

my long hair, but I did buy
$150 eye cream—just in case.

She also called to go over
the location of her will and

her funeral plans—
for the 843rd time. Yes, I know

the will is in the center drawer
of the tall dresser and that

she wants to wear the sparkly
black pant suit she donned for

Joe's wedding 10 years ago, and that Lyle,
her hairdresser for three decades,

will style her hair and apply her make-up.
but I don't like to talk

about it, so I *mmmhmmm* my way
through the conversation. I did

the same when my partner brought up
life insurance, and I made him

choose the plan. I'm not ready to
die, but I'm ready to dye,

and the bolder my hair color,
the louder I scream that I'm not leaving

the Earth. Maybe when I let my hair
gray, I'll start to age gracefully.

But for now, I'm eyeing
different color swatches,

and I look to the sky
for inspiration.

Unplugged

His face twitched,
just muscle spasms,
his brain departed.

The room smells
of cotton balls and stiff linen.
 Breathe, I told myself,
because he couldn't.

Thinking of the gap between his teeth,
I stand by a strong oak casket,
lid closed, too many lilies,
one hand on my belly,
a kick inside of me.

Backwash

He walked slowly
in the middle of
painted lines on a
four-lane road—
palms facing down,
fingers fanned, dirty
blond hair days away
from being dreads, scraggly
beard a shade darker,
open flannel shirt, bird
chest that looked finely plucked—
near a yellow drive-thru
taco shop with red lettering
advertising their quesadillas
and burritos, and he was probably
the lead singer in a ska band,
or maybe a surfer; the air
smelled like
industrial glue as
light fell out of the sky
and I wondered if he
could taste my salted
bitterness and spice
as I continued driving
to soccer practice,
seatbelt tightly buckled.

January

January, even if your arms
are cold, I need you
to wrap them around me—

quiet the ocean roiling
in my stomach, stop me
from juggling hot coals, and soothe

my itchy skin. *Please January,*
show me your clear
midnight sky, name

every constellation. My scream
is hushed as *I beg you, January,*
don't throw me off the bridge or light

my eyelashes on fire.
Put some music on, place me
in the bathtub and let me decide…

My house continues to shake.

Anxiety

I stare out of my office window
waiting for my tea to steep,
watching a woman sitting on
a red metal chair at a matching table,
her right leg furiously tapping while
my hair grays. My hair grays
while she listens to music
pumping through her ear buds—
piano notes to calm her or
maybe untamed guitar riffs
that mirror the bounce in her leg. She enjoys
the fresh air, her laptop lid closed,
while my hair grays and I
intrude in her life, if only
for a moment. My hair grays
while I think of my son
and how at age 16, he swallows
Prozac each night so he can
walk through the halls
of his high school, his eyes not
glued to the cheap linoleum floor.
I sip my tea and curl my long
strands around my index finger and decide
to pluck out every last gray.

Butterfly in the Window

Every day, I hold
      my breath.

In the windowsill, a stained glass butterfly. Catching light.

Made by my son in a second-grade classroom, it looks different
every time I wash dishes. Sometimes the red
is garnet, other times pink. The yellow
spreads on the white wall and late
in the day, it shrinks.

Like washing wool in hot water,
      I wither a little each August.
He grows—up to my nose,
and I blink and he's a whole head
      above me.

At the light of the day, he takes flight:
undeclared major, unexplored town.

Still, I see freckles on his face,
eyes reflecting the light of a butterfly,
and he moves a stray hair back in place.

Combat Hunger

I didn't even know
where I was walking. The smell
of orange chicken woke me out
of my daze, but then I
remembered that I'm on a
diet, that I can never be
thin enough, and my mind
returns to a picture
of me in a blue dress,
me too wide next to two
tiny women. I see a
sign, *Combat Hunger.*
Was this sign
for me?

Guide Words

Your number is still in my phone. I can't
call you and hear your voice,
slight Canadian accent
only sometimes.

Yet I'm closer to you each day
but still far—guide words
at the top of a dictionary page

that I can't turn forward or back.
I don't know what happened to us—
an apology over an email, I accepted,

before you left. I didn't
get the chance to say goodbye
and refused to look at you

lifeless in the oak casket, surrounded

by lilies and mums. I feel the weather
changing, a warm fall

settles in my bones,
or maybe a second summer.

Memory by Scent

Sitting under a pine tree
in the grass, my son plays
with a plastic sphere, trying to move
a tiny steel ball through
a maze, his tongue out
as he concentrates. A daughter
pushes her mother
in a wheelchair next to
the park, and they both
smile at us, the same
smile, from the same
face, one with deeper
wrinkles and wiser
eyes. I wonder if the mother
is from the memory care center
across the street and if a twilight
walk is their evening routine.
Their smiles tell me the story
of why the nursing home
was built next to a place
filled with the cracks
of baseball bats and children's
shrieks when they are caught
playing tag. I start
to count my son's
eyelashes, and I name
all five freckles on the right
side of his face. Without warning,
the lone pine smells like an entire forest.

Betsy Littrell is a quirky and creative soccer mom to four boys who recently found time to earn her MFA in Creative Writing. When she's not writing (or when she is), she enjoys a good cup of tea, a glass of rosé and peaceful moments by the beach with a book in hand. Having grown up in Massachusetts, she is a passionate and superstitious Red Sox fan and also cheers for Liverpool soccer with her partner, who makes her laugh like nobody else can. Her first full-length collection, *This Woman is Haunted*, was published in 2020, and her work has appeared in several journals.

www.ingramcontent.com/pod-product-compliance
Lightning Source LLC
LaVergne TN
LVHW041515070426
835507LV00012B/1600